Regulation Crowdfunding

Table of Contents

Title III of the JOBS Act added Section 4(6) to the Securities Act to provide an exemption from the registration provisions of the Securities Act for crowdfunding transactions involving the offering of securities, and added Section 4A to the Securities Act to set forth the requirements for issuers and intermediaries, liability provisions, and certain other matters relating to crowdfunding. In addition, Title III amended various provisions of the Exchange Act in connection with the crowdfunding provisions.

The JOBS Act requires the Commission to adopt a number of rules implementing crowdfunding, including the following:

1. Rules to carry out Section 4(6) and Section 4A of the Securities Act, pursuant to Section 302(c) of the JOBS Act;

2. Rules to provide for disqualifications of issuers, brokers or funding portals pursuant to Section 302(d) of the JOBS Act;

3. Rules to exempt, conditionally or unconditionally, the requirement for a registered funding portal to register as a broker or dealer under Section 15(a)(1) of the Exchange

Act, pursuant to Section 304(a) of the JOBS Act; andU.S. Securities and Exchange Commission;

4. Rules to exempt, conditionally or unconditionally, securities acquired in crowdfunding transactions from the scope of Section 12(g) of the Exchange Act, pursuant to Section 303 (b) of the JOBS Act.

In addition, Title III authorizes the Commission to adopt such additional rules as may be appropriate to implement the crowdfunding provisions under Title III.

This is the first issue of a monthly chronicle summarizing and commenting on Regulation Crowdfunding; we are initially relying heavily on comments submitted to date by the .Federal Regulation of Securities Committee of the Business Law Section of the American Bar Association.

Proposed Rules Governing Intermediaries

Risk of Fraud

Securities Act Section 4 A (a) (5) requires intermediaries to "take such measures to reduce the risk of fraud with respect to [transactions made in reliance on Section 4(a) (6) of the Securities Act], as established by the U. S. Securities and Exchange Commission (the Commission), by rule, including obtaining a background and enforcement regulatory history check on each officer, director, and person holding more than 20 percent of the outstanding equity of every issuer whose securities are offered by such person."

In other words, the Commission proposes that intermediaries need merely reasonably believe issuers are in compliance. Although intermediaries may not just rely on issuers' representations, they only need to have a reasonable basis to believe issuers are in compliance and this reasonable belief can be grounded merely on the representations of issuers unless there is reason to question them.

Current comment letters, understandably, point out that permitting such reliance is inconsistent with the Commission's Proposing Release as to the methods by which intermediaries can establish a reasonable belief as to compliance. Indeed, the text of the proposed rule provides a direct incentive for intermediaries *not* to check on issuers' compliance. As others have pointed out, having no reason to question a representation is not the same thing as reasonably relying on it.

Worse, the proposed rule permits intermediaries to claim the requisite belief based on prospective issuers clicking a button stating "I agree" to the terms of the engagement in the online application, without any assurance that issuers have actually read the terms when they so click. Everyone knows that most users, when presented with a so-called "click-through" agreement on a website, do not actually read the terms of whatever agreement is before them. When those terms include representations as to an issuer's compliance, issuers will almost certainly click the "I agree" button without reading the terms. Not only will the intermediaries not be required to take further due diligence, they will be incentivized not to make any further investigation so as to avoid learning anything that would lead them to question the issuers' compliance.

Accordingly, as a number of published comment letters posit, the Commission will undoubtedly apply the flexibility and the safe harbor provisions under Rule 506(c), or something similar, in lieu of what it now proposes.

Safe Harbors

Section 3(h)(1) of the Exchange Act directs the Commission to exempt registered funding portals from registration as broker/dealers because even their limited permitted activities can bring them within the definition of "broker." Clearly, funding portals acting as intermediaries in Section 4(a) (6)-exempt transactions are "effecting transactions in securities for the account of others by ensuring that investors comply with the conditions of Securities Act Section 4A (a) (4), and by making securities available for purchase, and by ensuring the proper transfer of funds and securities as required by Securities Act Section 4 A (a) (7)."

A funding portal's receipt of compensation tied to successful completion of a crowdfunding offering is also suggestive of its being a broker. In defining the term "funding portal," Congress imposed restrictions on the services that funding portals can provide without registering as a broker or dealer. New Exchange Act Section 3(a) (80) defines a funding portal as a person or entity that does not "(A) offer investment advice or recommendations; (B) solicit purchases, sales or offers to buy the securities offered or displayed on its website or portal; (C) compensate employees, agents, or other persons for such solicitation or based on the sale of securities displayed or referenced on its website or portal; (D) hold, manage, possess, or otherwise handle investor funds or securities; or (E) engage in such other activities as the Commission, by rule, determines appropriate."

Since merely making securities available for purchase through the portal can be deemed to involve solicitations, the Commission posits the non-exclusive safe harbor of proposed Rule 402, repeating Section 3(a) (80)'s prohibitions, and suggests a range of permissible portal activities, including activities that otherwise would likely be prohibited by Section 3(a) (80)).

The most recent comment letter of the Federal Regulation of Securities Committee of the Business Law Section of the American Bar Association (the ABA) also suggests that the Commission extend safe harbor coverage to the portal obligation to decide whether to deny an issuer access if it does not meet the portal's "objective" eligibility criteria or if the portal believes "that the issuer or the offering presents the potential for fraud or otherwise raises concerns regarding investor protection" for purposes of proposed Rule 301(c). Absent such protection, a portal, in making such "curatorial" determinations, will clearly be acting in an investment capacity function.

The same ABA comment letter also argues that the safe harbor standard should allow portals to evaluate offerings made on their platform with the "objective criteria" disclosed on portals' websites and that, "to be meaningful, the safe harbor should be supplemented by explicit Commission guidance – preferably in the regulatory text -- that a portal engaging in activities covered by proposed Rule 402(b) will not trigger the application of the Investment Advisers Act of 1940."

Other published comment letters have suggested that the Commission provide specific guidance, preferably in regulatory text, regarding what investor protection concerns should lead a portal to reject an offering. It is also important that the portal warn investors that the fact that it may reject offerings does not proffer any assurance of investor protection.

Compensation and Unanswered Questions

Proposed compensatory rules do not allow portals to pay transaction-based compensation to a third party for investor or issuer referrals unless that third party is a registered broker-dealer. The portal may not receive transaction-based compensation for referring potential investors in exempt offerings other than Section 4(a) (6)-exempt transactions being effected by a registered broker-dealer.

Still, it remains unclear when compensation paid by a portal to a third party other than a registered broker-dealer will be deemed improperly to "be based, directly or indirectly, on the purchase or sale of a security offered in reliance on Section 4(a) (6) on or through the portal's platform." Another unanswered question is the extent to which portals may pay initiating brokers for referrals. Finally, it remains unclear whether a funding portal may charge fees that are tied to the success of a specific offering.

Advertising

Proposed Rule 402(b)(9) permits funding portals to engage in limited advertising and to identify the offerings available at their platforms. Such advertisements must be based on objective criteria such as the type of securities offered, geographic location, industry or business sector, and the interest of investors measured by number of investment commitments. The portals are barred, in short, from receiving compensation that may affect their judgment. While the example in the proposed regulatory text and discussed in the Proposing Release 30 provide helpful guidance, the Commission has yet to clarify the limitations of advertising or to clarify whether emails promoting investments sent by a funding portal to potential investors (who presumably have signed up with that portal to receive emails) would be considered "advertising" and subject to the limitations set out in the safe harbor.

It should be noted that so-called "passive bulletin boards," not registered as broker-dealers, are currently sending emails recommending investment in particular companies. While such activity may comply with SEC no-action letters authorizing such bulletin board's operations, without Exchange Act registration as a broker-dealer or a securities exchange, funding portals who follow this practice do so at their peril.

Proposed Rules Governing Capital Raises and the Integration Doctrine

Capital Raises

Commentators to date have generally agreed that the Commission's overall approach to the amount of capital that an issuer may raise pursuant to the Section 4(a)(6) exemption is practicable and appropriate. The Commission obviously recognizes that issuers will be discouraged from attempted to rely on Regulation Crowdfunding if the statutory $1 million cap is effectively lessened through aggregation with crowdfunding proceeds of amounts raised in non-crowdfunding transactions conducted in reliance upon other Securities Act exemptions.

In other words, the Commission recognizes that amounts raised in exempt offerings conducted under Section 4(a)(6) should not be aggregated with amounts raised in other exempt offerings by the same or affiliated issuers during the preceding 12 months for purposes of determining the $1 million cap. And the Commission has acknowledges that as long as an offering complies with the requirements of the particular exemption that is being relied upon for that particular offering – *whether that exemption is Section 4(a)(6), Section 4(a)(2) and/or Rule 506(b), Rule 506(c), Regulation A, and/or any other available exemption* – there is no reason to aggregate amounts.

Accordingly, the doctrine of integration will not integrate Section 4(a)(6) offerings with other exempt offerings by the same issuer or affiliated issuers conducted either concurrently or consecutively within any given 12 month period.

What the Commission is proposing is consistent with the intention of Section 4(a)(6); to wit, "to provide an additional mechanism for capital raising by startup and small businesses….," by enabling "[a]n issuer … [to] complete an offering that is made in reliance on Section 4(a)(6) that occurs simultaneously with, or is preceded or followed by, another exempt offering."

The Commission's decision that "offerings made in reliance on Section 4(a)(6) should not necessarily be integrated with other exempt offerings if the conditions to the applicable exemptions are met" is arguably the right decision (at least from an issuer's point of view!). Footnote 33 of the Proposing Release sets forth ine way an issuer conducting concurrent crowdfunding and Rule 506(b)-exempt offerings may satisfy itself that a prospective investor in the Rule 506(b) private offering did not become interested in a private investment as a result of the "public" exempt offering made in reliance upon Section 4(a)(6).

The ability of small issuers to rely on other Securities Act exemptions, especially those facilitating private offerings, will enable fundraising from more sophisticated investors whose financial acumen can serve to enhance the protections of crowdfunding investors, or at least that is the view of the ABA.

Still, it may be difficult for small, development-stage issuers to answer some of the more complex questions posed in the Commission's requests for comment without additional guidance from the Commission. For example, it is not clear when general solicitation/general advertising activities undertaken in connection with a Rule 506(c)-exempt offering will be deemed to have been conducted "in a manner that is intended, or could reasonably be expected to, condition the market for a [concurrent or subsequent] Section 4(a)(6) offering or generate referrals to a crowdfunding intermediary." Nor is it clear whether the limited advertising permitted in Section 4(a)(6) offerings pursuant to an intermediary's electronic platform will be treated as general solicitation or advertising that might taint a simultaneous exempt offering under Section 4(a)(2) and/or Rule 506(b).

The Commission does not want to restrict an issuer from offering securities under Section 4(a)(6) within a specified period before, after or contemporaneously with another exempt offering. Similarly, it does not want to impose restrictions or conditions on a non-crowdfunding exemption that would not otherwise apply in the absence of a concurrent or consecutive crowdfunding transaction pursuant to Section 4(a)(6). Accordingly, the ABA's latest comment letter pleads with the Commission to articulate "a simple, principles-based analytical framework that would help smaller issuers identify and address integration questions on a case-by-case basis."

An issuer that begins an offering under Section 4(a)(6) should be able to convert that offering to a Rule 506(c) offering. In other words, an offer made under Section 4(a)(6) should not preclude an offer made by means of general solicitation or advertising in reliance upon Rule 506(c) shortly thereafter, provided of course that all purchasers in the Rule 506(c)-exempt offering are accredited investors and that the required "reasonable steps to verify" have been undertaken. The following is a model "Verification Letter:"

MODEL LETTER: ACCREDITED INVESTOR VERIFICATION

[Date]

[Client name and address]

Reference: Letter of Accredited Investor Verification

Dear Sir/Madame:

[Client name] ("Client") has asked Private Placement Advisors LLC to confirm that Client has taken reasonable steps to determine that [name of investor] ("Investor") is an accredited investor as defined in Rule 501(a) under the Securities Act of 1933.

Client understands that the SEC has not yet offered either a uniform verification method or a non-comprehensive list of verification methods to satisfy the verification requirement. Client acknowledges that a determination of whether the verification steps taken in a given transaction are "reasonable" are grounded in the particular facts and circumstances surrounding each transaction.

Client understands that the determination of whether a person is an accredited investor is a factual question to which a legal opinion does not obtain nor apply.

Client understands that in addition to the minimum income and net worth requirements, the Client needs to consider the type of Investor and the amount and type of information that the Client has about the Investor. Client understands that the more information that it has indicating that an Investor is accredited, the fewer steps will be necessary to verify any Investor's eligibility.

Client understands that the methods through which it has publicly solicited investors through general advertising may be relevant in determining the reasonableness of the steps it takes to verify accredited investor status. For instance, an issuer that solicits new investors through a website accessible to the general public, or through social media solicitation, will be required to undertake more stringent verification steps than an issuer that solicits investors from a database of "screened" accredited investors maintained by a "reasonably reliable" third-party.

Client further understands that the terms of an offering may be relevant. For example, setting a high minimum investment amount requirement per investor, especially with a direct cash investment that is not financed, so that only accredited investors could reasonably be expected to risk losing their entire investment, further verifies accredited investor status.

Client further understands that the Client bears the burden of establishing the availability of an SEC Regulation D exemption. Private Placement Advisors LLC does not make any representation about whether this letter is sufficient for Client's purposes.

This confirms that Client has reviewed the original or copies of the following documents:

1. Joint tax returns for the years 2012 and 2013 (each a "Tax Year") filed by Client and [his/her] spouse on Form 1040 (the "Tax Returns"), accompanied by a certificate signed by the Client, attached hereto and addressed to us, attesting that the copies of the Tax Returns provided are true, correct and complete, filed with the appropriate office of the Internal Revenue Service, prepared in full compliance with applicable law and governmental regulations and have not been amended;

2. A certificate executed by Client and [his/her] spouse, attached hereto, and addressed to us, stating such persons have a reasonable expectation of joint income in the current year in excess of $300,000.

Private Placement Advisors LLC has not conducted any other investigation or inquiries of Client, and has not determined whether the Tax Returns were accurately prepared, or agree with source documents, or were properly filed. This letter is limited to the matters set forth herein and speaks only as of the date hereof. Nothing may be inferred or implied beyond the matters expressly contained herein.

This confirms [fact pattern that applies to steps taken to determine accredited investor status].

Based on the totality of the information provided, it is the opinion of Private Placement Advisors LLC that Client has taken reasonable steps to establish that Investor is an accredited investor under SEC Regulation D.

Private Placement Advisors LLC is qualified to provide this opinion based on its managing partner's professional qualifications.

This letter may be relied upon by Client only in connection with an offering under Rule 506(c) and only for 30 days from the date of this letter. This letter may not be used, quoted from, referred to or relied upon by you or by any other person for any other purpose, nor may copies be delivered to any other person, without in each instance express prior written consent of Private Placement Advisors LLC.

Client understands that the Securities Exchange Commission requires verification every 90 days as Rule 506(c)'s application regulations are now being interpreted.

Cordially,

Private Placement Advisors LLC

By: _____
Douglas Slain
Managing Partner

Individual Investment Limitations

The Commission's interpretation of Section 4(a)(6)(B) will, in one instance, impose an overall investment ceiling of $100,000 and, for issuers within that ceiling, provide a "greater of" limitation based on an investor's annual income or net worth. This is a good thing because a more restrictive reading of the JOBS Act's ambiguous language would unduly hinder small issuer capital formation without doing anything to protect investors. An investor with more limited resources will not be permitted to invest more than the greater of $2,000 or 5 percent of annual income or net worth, if both his or her annual income and net worth are less than $100,000.

[Author's Note: The following language is heavily borrowed, albeit with substantial editing, from the ABA's latest comment letter.]

Offerings of $100,000 or Less within a Twelve-Month Period

"[s]trong privacy policy considerations warrant the omission of "personally identifiable information," including . . . Social Security numbers, from the issuer tax returns for the most recent fiscal year that must be filed . . . and provided to investors and the relevant intermediary . . with offerings of $100,000 or less. [w]e recommend that the Commission include . . . a non-exhaustive list of the specific types of information that may be redacted. "[b]ecause GAAP are "generally self-scaling to the size and complexity of the issuer," the burden of preparing financial statements may be reduced for some smaller issuers."
"[s]tart-ups without an operating history . . . will be unable to make use of the Section 4(a)(6) exemption because they lack the resources to hire employees with the financial or accounting expertise necessary to prepare GAAP-compliant financial statements.
Moreover, there may be some risk that crowdfunding issuers incurring an ongoing reporting obligation under proposed Rule 202 – like issuers tapping Tier 2 of Regulation A, if adopted as proposed by the Commission – may be viewed by the Financial Accounting Standards Board ("FASB") as "public business entities" that may not qualify for less burdensome private company alternatives available under GAAP." " . . .[w]e do not believe that this and any other benefits associated with GAAP-compliant financial statements outweigh the burdens that

mandatory application of GAAP would impose on many newly formed or development-stage issuers with a promising business idea that desperately need seed capital, but are unable for whatever reason to attract the interest of venture capital firms or even angel investors." " . . .

"[m]any issuers . . . might not have any financial history, and potential investors might make investment decisions without a track record of issuer performance, relying largely on the belief that an issuer can succeed based on the concept and other factors."

"To compel these [small] issuers to produce up to two years' . . . of financial statements GAAP prescribes would . . . eliminate a Section 4(a)(6)-exempt offering as a viable capital-raising alternative for these issuers. " . . [c]urrent Regulation A, as well as proposed Regulation A Tier 1 (up to $5 million/12 months) and Tier 2 (up to $50 million/12 months), call for financial statements presented in accordance with GAAP. Nevertheless, the cost-benefit calculus of a small issuer with no revenues and/or minimal assets that seeks a maximum of $100,000 within a twelve-month period from the "crowd," through an intermediary that must be paid for its services, is far different than that of a small issuer seeking as much as $5 million from investors on a disintermediated basis over the same period. " . . .

"[w]e urge the Commission to . . . consider providing conditional relief from . . . GAAP compliance for small issuers seeking no more than $100,000 . . . within a given twelve-month period." "[n]ewly formed issuers or issuers with no operating history and/or revenues should be permitted to prepare financial statements covering whatever period they have been in existence using a comprehensive basis of accounting other than GAAP (e.g., income tax basis, cash basis, modified cash basis)."
" . . .[t]he Commission could require the issuer's certifying principal executive officer to represent that the issuer is unable to prepare financial statements in accordance with GAAP without unreasonable effort or expense (see, in this regard, the Commission's Request for

Comment No. 66) because it has not yet generated revenue and otherwise has no access to funding . . . " Of course, an issuer could be required to provide GAAP-compliant financial statements if available..

Offerings of More Than $100,000 But Not More Than $500,000 Within a Twelve-Month Period.

"w]e have recommended that . . . smaller issuers raising no more than $100,000 . . . be given . . . relief from the obligation to . . . file . . . GAAP-compliant financial statements under cover of Form C. Similar relief would be appropriate . . . for some issuers that conduct offerings that fall into the middle statutory tier . . . of more than $100,000 . . . up to $500,000 . . ."

" . . .[t]he Commission has . . . has enabled crowdfunding issuers to provide financial statements reviewed by an independent public accountant in accordance with the Statements on Standards for Accounting and Review Services ('SSARS') promulgated by the Accounting and Review Services Committee . . .".

"Under the SSARS, an independent auditor may conduct an audit or review of financial statements prepared in conformity with a comprehensive basis of accounting other than GAAP or International Financial Reporting Standards ("IFRS"). Section 4A(b)(1)(D)(ii) not only enables the Commission to designate . . . a SSARS as the appropriate review framework . . . but also permits the Commission to determine that GAAP-compliant financial statements may not be necessary . . . for all offerings by all crowdfunding issuers whose Section 4(a)(6)-exempt offerings bring them within this middle statutory tier. " . . [t]he Commission should consider allowing small issuers raising up to $500,000 . . . to provide financial statements that have been prepared on an acceptable basis other than GAAP – referred to by the AICPA as Other Comprehensive Basis of Accounting or "OCBOA" – and reviewed by an independent public accounting firm . . ."

"An issuer's ability to provide such financial statements could be limited to situations in which the issuer has no operating history and/or revenues, and/or a minimal amount of assets as measured in terms of dollar value (e.g., assets worth less than $500,000), and has not prepared GAAP-compliant financial statements for any other purpose." "[t]he Commission could require the issuer's principal executive officer to certify that financial statements could not be presented in accordance with GAAP without unreasonable expense and other burdens."

" . . [w]e support the Commission's determination to apply the independence standards set forth in Rule 2-01 of Regulation S-X. While application of these standards . . . 'may impose higher costs than other independence standards, such as the AICPA standards,' the Commission could consider mitigation of these costs for certain smaller issuers that lack the resources to prepare financial statements in accordance with GAAP . . ."

Offerings of More Than $500,000 (But No More than $1Million) Within a Twelve-Month Period

" . . .[G]iven what we believe will be the substantial costs for many start-ups of obtaining an audit by an accounting firm that passes muster under Rule 2-01 of Regulation S-X,15 . . . we urge the Commission to exercise the authority Congress conferred in Section 4A(b)(1)(D)(iii) to raise the $500,000 threshold to $750,000."

"We agree with the Commission's statement that 'audited financial statements would benefit investors in offerings by issuers with substantive prior business activity by providing them with greater confidence in the quality of the financial statements of issuers seeking to raise larger amounts of capital." The . . .question . . . is whether the perceived investor benefits of an audit are outweighed by the costs to smaller non-reporting issuers in situations where the amount of capital sought within a twelve-month period exceeds $500,000." "[i]t is likely that more developed private issuers with operating track records will eschew crowdfunding in favor of using Rule 506(b) or (c), for which no audited financial statements are prescribed (and no offering amount ceiling is imposed), so long as all sales are made to the type of 'accredited investor' that these issuers would be better able to attract. By contrast, those 'newly formed' issuers, with little or no operations – clearly among the intended beneficiaries of Title III – are more likely to conclude . . .that 'the benefit of the audit may not justify the cost of the audit,' and . . . decide against seeking more than $500,000 in much-needed capital under Section 4(a)(6).

"A review of the required financial statements in accordance with AICPA standards by an independent accounting firm qualified under S-X Rule 2-01 is sufficient, in our view, to protect investors without unduly discouraging those smaller, startup issuers that are not yet profitable from utilizing the new crowdfunding exemption . . ." "Moreover, we recommend that the Commission . . . go beyond the text of Section 4A(b)(1)(D)(iii) to require that all issuer financial statements for offerings covered by this statutory tier be prepared in accordance with GAAP."

"Newly formed, family-owned businesses whose management have no intention of ever "going public" in the traditional sense might wish to use crowdfunding as a seed capital mechanism, but would be deterred by the significant costs and other burdens attendant to GAAP compliance (whether these costs are analyzed alone or in conjunction with the costs of obtaining an audit). In addition to lacking an operating and/or financial track record, such businesses might have little or no cash flow and minimal assets."

"Both for these small issuers, and for . . . 'friends-and-family' investors who want to support a promising new business concept via direct investment, the costs of producing GAAP-compliant financial statements may far outweigh any perceived benefits."

"By not prescribing GAAP-compliant financial statements for any of the statutory offering tiers, including the top tier, the framers of Section 4A(b)(1)(D) arguably intended to give these issuers a shot at beating the odds via crowdfunding regardless of the amounts they are trying to raise (subject to the $1 million/12-month limitation)." " . . [w]e ask the Commission to consider allowing some issuers seeking more than $500,000 within twelve months – for example, those start-ups with no operating history or revenue, and minimal assets – to provide financial statements presented on a comprehensive basis other than GAAP if the principal executive officer can certify that the issuer is unable to prepare financial statements in accordance with GAAP without undue cost and other burden, and that the OCBOA methodology selected is acceptable under AICPA audit standards."

Proposed Rules Governing Issuer Disclosures
Non-Financial Disclosure Requirements

Description of Business and Business Plan

Proposed Rule 201(d) of Regulation Crowdfunding requires issuers to submit a copy of their business plan in addition to a description of their business. The Commission has suggested that it does not expect issuers to provide either "a document prepared by management for internal use only" or "a marketing document used to solicit investors," both of which have been understandably described by commenters as forms of business plans. *So what does the Commission expect?* Comment letters to the Commission on this subject are rife with wonder.

Although a discussion of an issuer's business and a business plan have much in common, generally a business plan is more subject to ongoing updating. *Because most issuers will be in the early stages of their business, it is unclear how finalized their business plans will be at the time they most need to raise capital.*

Moreover, to the extent that such early-stage issuers do have relatively final business plans, these plans are still likely to be subject to numerous small and large re-iterations as time goes along. Also, the proposed business plan disclosure requirement appears to overlap with the proposed requirement in proposed Rule 201(i)) calling for a description of the purpose and intended use of the offering proceeds. Accordingly, the latest ABA comment letter suggests that the Commission eliminate the proposed requirement to disclose a business plan prior to an offering and, instead, require crowdfunding issuers to describe their proposed business as well as the purpose and intended use of the proceeds being solicited. The ABA also suggests that the Commission publish a non-exclusive list of what will constitute material items, such as the types of information regarding their plan of operations specified in Item 101(a)(2) of Regulation S-K. The ABA argues that the absence of a "specific idea or business plan" should not disqualify an issuer from using the Section 4(a)(6) exemption as implemented by Regulation Crowdfunding. An issuer whose sole business purpose is to engage in a merger or acquisition involving an unidentified company or companies should not be eligible to use the crowdfunding mechanism. But that does not mean that a particular business idea disclosed by a crowdfunding issuer should be deemed after-the-fact—either by the Commission's staff or by disappointed investors—to be too non-specific to permit reliance on Section 4(a)(6), thus exposing that issuer to the truly draconian consequences of a Section 5 violation.

The ABA also asserts, "[s]ome of the Commission's proposed disclosure requirements go beyond what is required by Section 4A(b) of the Securities Act and therefore may impose inappropriate burdens on smaller issuers. Thus, while "Section 4A(b)(1)(I) specifies that the Commission may require additional disclosures for the protection of investors and in the public interest," the Commission should give careful consideration to whether such disclosures are necessary or appropriate to protect investors."

Compelling some disclosures could have the unintended consequence of discouraging issuers from relying on Regulation Crowdfunding to raise capital.

For instance, proposed Rule 201(b) requires issuers to disclose the business experience of each director and officer for the preceding three years. Although this is less than the five-year period under the "old" Regulation A, that regulation has a $5 million/12-month ceiling compared to the $1 million/12-month ceiling proposed for a Regulation Crowdfunding offering. Other commentators have observed that the required disclosure of names of each officer, director and greater-than-20%-share holders (along with the proposed disqualification provisions) provide sufficient protection. For this reason, the ABA urges the Commission to limit the business experience disclosure requirement to one year. Proposed Rule 201(f), if adopted, would require issuers to discuss the material factors that make investment in a particular issuer speculative or risky. Item 2 to General Instruction II of proposed Form C also would require inclusion of the following legend: "*A crowdfunding investment involves a risk. You should not invest any funds in this offering unless you can afford to lose your entire investment.*"

All that is required by Section 4A(b) is disclosure of "the risks to purchasers of the securities relating to minority ownership in the issuer, the risks associated with corporate actions, including additional issuances of shares, a sale of the issuer or of assets of the issuer, or transactions with related parties." Disclosure of the risks detailed in the statute, along with the proposed legend, is arguably all that should be required of issuers seeking to rely on the crowdfunding exemption.

Financial Disclosures

The Commission has proposed that issuers include in offering materials a narrative discussion of their financial condition similar to the management discussion and an analysis of financial condition and results of operations ("MD&A") disclosure required in registered offerings, as well as a tiered financial statement disclosure. These requirements increase in complexity and detail as the amount to be raised exceeds certain monetary thresholds

The Commission has taken an admirably flexible approach to financial disclosures, predicated on materiality. However, this author strongly agrees with the latest published ABA comment letter recommending against the imposition of public company style "MD&A" disclosure obligations on small companies, as Instruction to Rule 201(s) would have it.

First, there is little precedent to guide the management of a private company in assessing how a "reasonable investor" can be expected to deal with such disclosures. Second, there is the following problematic instruction: " For issuers with no prior operating history, the description should include, to the extent reasonably known, a discussion of financial milestones and operational, liquidity and other challenges." (Proposing Release at 66553 [regulatory text of proposed Rule 201(s)]). For issuers with no prior operating history and often little practical or legal knowledge or experience, it will particularly hard to discern what should be "reasonably known." Third, there should not be a duty to disclose "known events, trends and uncertainties," as required of public companies in the MD&A, in that such a responsibility will be unusually difficult for inexperienced start-up companies. Fourth, again the author agrees with ABA's latest comment letter suggesting "an illustrative, non-prescriptive list of Questions and Answers that management could consider in drafting the financial condition discussion." As noted, Questions 47 through 50 of Form 1-A (Model A), used in current Regulation A offerings, provide the needed template, at least for companies with an operating history.

Proposed Rules Governing Reporting Requirements

Section 4A(b)(4) instructs the Commission to determine how crowdfunding issuers should meet the statutory mandate to file with the Commission and to provide investors, "not less than annually[,] ... reports of the results of operations and financial statements of the issuer, ... subject to such exceptions and termination dates as the Commission may establish by rule." *This provision may turn out to be unduly burdensome for those issuers most likely to engage in crowdfunding transactions.* Most crowdfunding issuers will be smaller companies, with minimal or no operations and will lack access to legal and financial talent necessary to comply with the annual reporting obligation.

The ABA has suggested that, "[t]hat the requisite financial statements (both content and outside review/audit elements) for annual reporting purposes should be proportionate to the aggregate amount actually raised within a twelve-month period in reliance upon Section

4(a)(6). For this reason, we believe that GAAP-compliant financials should not be required on an ongoing basis for certain issuers that raise $500,000 or less under Section 4(a)(6) within that period."

The ABA has also argued that an audit of an issuer's financial statements should not be required unless an issuer has raised more than, say, $750,000 under Section 4(a)(6) within a twelve-month period. The same rationale applies to the issuer's choice of accounting frameworks for its ensuing annual financial statements, at least according to, again, the ABA's latest comment letter.

The ABA writes, ... "[c]onsistent with the arguments outlined above with respect to financial disclosures prescribed for crowdfunding offerings, we believe that the requisite financial statements (both content and outside review/audit elements) for annual reporting purposes should be proportionate to the aggregate amount actually raised within a twelve-month period in reliance upon Section 4(a)(6). For this reason, we believe that GAAP-compliant financials should not be required on an ongoing basis for certain issuers that raise $500,000 or less under Section 4(a)(6) within that period. And there are some limited circumstances, as discussed above, in which an issuer that has raised more than $500,000 in exempt crowdfunding transactions over a twelve-month period should be permitted to file both offering-related and annual financial statements that have been prepared on a comprehensive basis of accounting other than GAAP." " . . . [i]ssuers that raise $100,000 or less under Section 4(a)(6) should be excepted from future ongoing filing obligations after filing one annual report on Form C-AR.

Proposed Rules Governing Issuer Advertising

The Commission proposes to implement Section 4A(b)(2)'s prohibition against issuer advertising with proposed Rule 204 of Regulation Crowdfunding. Comment letters are persuasively arguing for an exception to allow issuers to continue to publish regularly released factual business information – whether on an issuer's website or elsewhere – so long as such communications do not refer to the terms of the offering. (Proposing Release at 66437: "We believe that an 'online-only' requirement enables the public to access offering information and share information in a way that will allow members of the crowd to decide whether or not to participate in the offering and fund the business or idea." Also, "[T]he intermediary would only need to post the [issuer's offering-related] information on its platform in a manner complying with proposed Rule 303(a) and would not be required to send any electronic messages with regard to its posting.").

As the Commission observes, "[p]ermitting [crowdfunding] issuers to continue to engage in communications that do not refer to the terms of the offering during the pendency of [an] offering made in reliance on Section 4(a)(6) would increase the likelihood of the success of an issuer's business because the issuer could continue to advertise its products or services, so long as it does so without discussing the terms of the offering."

The Commission is expected to provide guidance as to how to respond to unsolicited inquiries regarding ongoing crowdfunding offerings. Assumedly, an issuer may respond to such inquiries by providing the information contained in the Notice, directing inquiries to the intermediary's platform.

Proposed Rules Governing Re-Sales

Comment letters to date (June 9, 2014) uniformly concur that the provisions of proposed Rule 501 are sufficient to Implement Section 4A(e)'s restrictions on resale of securities issued under Section 4(a)(6). Rule 144A re-sales to qualified institutional buyers ("QIBs") will also be Permitted during this one-year period, as the statute allows re-sales to "accredited investors" and the QIB eligibility criteria exceed those of accredited investors as defined in Rule 501(a) of Regulation D. For similar reasons, bona fide offshore re-sales under Rule 904 of Regulation S almost certainly will be permissible during the one-year period.

Once the Section 4A(e) one-year limitation on transfers has expired, securities originally issued in a Section 4(a)(6)-exempt offering will be able to be re-sold pursuant to Section 4(a)(1) and/or the Rule 144, Rule 144A or Regulation S safe harbor – provided the conditions to reliance on the particular exemption or exemptive safe harbor are still met. As the latest ABA comment letter asserts, "[T]he current public information" requirement of Rule 144(c) and the 'current information' requirement of Rule 144A(d)(4) should be deemed to be met if the crowdfunding issuer has complied with ongoing reporting obligations."

Proposed Rules Governing Disqualifications and Waivers

Since the Commission adopted the final rule regarding the disqualification of "bad actors" with Rule 506 offerings, a number of interpretative questions have arisen. Thus, while the Commission has provided helpful guidance on several issues through three sets of Compliance and Disclosure Interpretations, questions remain--such as, for example, the intended meaning of the term "voting securities." The ABA, among others, has asked that the Commission enact rules that—for purposes of the disqualification provisions applicable to exempt offerings conducted under Regulation Crowdfunding, as well as Regulations A and D—the term "voting securities" has the meaning ascribed to it under Exchange Act Rule 12b-2.

The Proposing Release would allow the Commission to waive disqualification under Proposed Rule 503, and it provides a few examples of circumstances that might justify a waiver.

Of course the costs associated with submitting a waiver request may deter eligible smaller issuers from undertaking a waiver request and therefore foreclose access to the crowdfunding marketplace.

Proposed Rules Governing Exemption from Section 12(g of the Exchange Act

There appears to be universal agreement the Commission's proposed rules governing Rule 12g-That will exclude from the definition of "held of record," for purposes of Section 12(g), those "securities issued pursuant to the offering exemption under Section 4(a)(6) of the Securities Act." As the ABA puts it, "[t]his isthe most logical and appropriate interpretation of Exchange Act Section 12(g)(6), which is consistent with the capital formation purposes of Securities Act Section 4(a)(6) and the inclusion of the Section 12(g) exemption in Title III rather than Title V, is to apply the Section 12(g) exemption to the securities issued in a Section 4(a)(6)-exempt crowdfunding offering, such that the Section 12(g) exemption continues to be available once the securities are sold or otherwise transferred by the initial purchaser of such securities. Unlike the Title V amendments focused on holders -- i.e., excluding only those holders who are 'accredited investors' and 'securities held by persons who received' the securities issued pursuant to an exempt offering by an employee compensation plan -- new Section 12(g)(6) references only the securities, and not a particular holder or class of holders. We think the most analogous provision is the definition of "restricted security" set forth in Securities Act Rule 144(a)(3), which encompasses "securities acquired" in a variety of exempt transactions and imposes resale restrictions and enables all subsequent holders to rely on its safe harbor, not just the person who initially acquired the securities in the initial exempt transaction."

As another commentator phrased it, "Were the Section 12(g) exemption limited to the initial purchaser of crowdfunding securities and certain related parties of the initial purchasers, the issuer would forever be exposed to a "springing" Section 12(g) reporting obligation, which could be triggered if the initial purchasers were to resell their equity securities, which may occur without the issuer's knowledge or involvement.

Although the suggested $25 million threshold may be viewed as overly restrictive, a company that no longer resembles a startup entity should not be entitled to the benefits of the Exchange Act exemption.

Proposed Rules Governing Statutory Liability of Portals

Most commentator agree that the applicability of Section 12(a)(2) to funding portals is not settled law at this time. For instance, *In Pinter v. Dahl, 486 U.S. 622, 642-648 (1988)*, the Supreme Court held that a person who is not passing title to the securities can be deemed to be a seller for purposes of liability under Section 12(a)(2) only to the extent the person solicits purchases or offers to purchase securities.

The Proposing Release did, however, express the view that because Section 4A(c)(3) defines "issuer" to include "any person who offers or sells the security in such offering," "it appears likely that intermediaries, including funding portals, would be considered issuers for purposes of this liability provision." In addition, the Commission has stated that, "[t]he anti-fraud and civil liability provisions of the Securities Act, such as Sections 12(a)(2) and apply to exempted transactions, including those transactions that will be conducted in reliance on Section 4(a)(6)."

As always, any person who solicits purchasers of securities in Section 4(a)(6) offerings is a seller subject to potential liability under Section 4A(c) and, as a consequence, firms and individuals intending to become a funding portal (even without intent to solicit purchasers) may well be deterred. For instance, what is a funding portal's obligation to perform due diligence beyond the regulatory "reasonable basis" obligation imposed by Section 4A(a)(5) (as well as proposed Rule 301)?

Of course, if funding portals cannot receive compensation for soliciting activities they cannot be subject to the same private liability as persons or entities who are compensated—that much is clear. And, as always, if an issuer makes an untrue statement of a material fact or omits to state a material fact required to be stated or necessary in order to make the statements, in light of the circumstances under which they were made, not misleading, and the purchaser did not know of the untruth or omission, liability obtains.

The Proposing Release does, however, express the Commission's view that because Section 4A(c)(3) defines "issuer" to include "any person who offers or sells the security in such Offering; therefore, "it appears likely that intermediaries, including funding portals, will be considered issuers for purposes of this liability provision." In addition, the Commission noted in a footnote to its discussion that "[t]he anti-fraud and civil liability provisions of the Securities Act, such as Sections 12(a)(2) and 17, apply to exempted transactions, including those transactions that will be conducted in reliance on Section 4(a)(6)."

It does not appear that a funding portal necessarily falls within the definition of "issuer" for purposes of Section 4A(c) liability. Among other reasons, funding portals are prohibited from "solicit[ing] purchases, sales, or offers to buy the securities offered or displayed on its website or portal" or "compensat[ing] employees, agents, or other persons for such solicitation."

Merely listing a security on its website (or by identifying a broad selection of issuers in its advertising), a funding portal would not be engaged in a solicitation of purchases or offers to buy securities. The consensus of opinion is that Congress did not intend that funding portals serve as selling agents, but rather simply as "neutral marketplaces."

As the ABA points out in its last comment letter, "[a]lthough the Senate amendments that became the crowdfunding provisions of the JOBS Act clearly intended to subject issuers and their officers and directors to a due diligence obligation, the same intent does not appear to extend to firms merely acting as portals. See, e.g., Cong. Rec. S1884 (daily ed. Mar. 21, 2012) "What the Senate bill says is, in order for this capital market to work well one has to stand behind the accuracy of their information. It has basic liability accountability; that is, as a director or officer of this organization, they are standing behind the accuracy of what they put out. It has a due diligence protection so this is very balanced." (Statement of Sen. Merkley). One commentator notes that under the Supreme Court's opinion in *Gustafson v. Alloyd Co., 513 U.S. 561 (1995)*, Section 12(a)(2) would apply to exempt public offerings, such as a crowdfunding transaction under Section 4(a)(6). The JOBS Act does make clear that persons dealing in securities pursuant to Section 3(b)(2) of the Securities Act are subject to Section 12(a)(2) liability. The specific language is: "An action brought under this paragraph shall be subject to the provisions of section 77l(b) of this title and section 77m of this title, as if the liability were created under section 77l(a)(2) of this title."

Highlights of Comments on Proposed Rules Regarding Financial Statements

Smaller issuers raising no more than $100,000 within a twelve-month

period should be given relief from the obligation to file GAAP-compliant

financial statements under cover of Form C.

Similar relief should be given issuers that conduct offerings of more than $100,000 up to and

including $500,000 within a given twelve-month period.

The Commission has already exercised its authority under the statute to enable crowdfunding

issuers to provide financial statements reviewed by an independent public accountant in

accordance with the Statements on Standards for Accounting and Review Services ("SSARS")

promulgated by the Accounting and Review Services Committee of the American Institute of

Certified Public Accountants ("AICPA").

Under the SSARS, an independent auditor may conduct an audit or review of financial statements prepared in conformity with a comprehensive basis of accounting other than GAAP or International Financial Reporting Standards ("IFRS").

Author

Doug was the secured transactions adviser to the Ministry of Economy for the Republic of Latvia and he taught as an adjunct law professor at Stanford Law School for one term. He also served as the chair of the American Bar Association's' General Practice Section's Professional Responsibility Committee for two terms.

Doug received a J.D. from Stanford Law School and practiced securities and business law at Pillsbury, Madion & Sutro. He later founded a law publishing company that published a number of monthly law reporting services, including *Insurance Litigation Reporter, Professional Liability Reporter, Construction Litigation Reporter,* and *Medical Liability Reporter,* titles eventually sold to McGraw-Hill and now published by Thomson-Reuters.

.